Supreme Being

Martha Kapos

Supreme Being

ENITHARMON PRESS

First published in 2008
by Enitharmon Press
26B Caversham Road
London NW5 2DU

www.enitharmon.co.uk

Distributed in the UK by
Central Books
99 Wallis Road
London E9 5LN

Distributed in the USA and Canada
by Dufour Editions Inc.
PO Box 7, Chester Springs
PA 19425, USA

ISBN: 978-1-904634-62-1

Enitharmon Press gratefully acknowledges the financial support of
Arts Council England, London.

British Library Cataloguing-in-Publication Data.
A catalogue record for this book is available
from the British Library.

Designed in Albertina by Libanus Press
and printed in England by
CPI Antony Rowe

ACKNOWLEDGEMENTS

Thanks are due to the editors of the following publications where these poems, sometimes in earlier versions, first appeared: *The Boy Under the Water* (The Many Press, 1989), *Cimarron Review, The Manhattan Review, Modern Poetry in Translation, Poetry London, PN Review, Poetry Review, Poetry Wales, A Room To Live In* (Salt, 2007).

CONTENTS

GUST

Nothing prepared me for the way you walked
on ahead and carried on with deliberate speed
until reaching your own last border you

stepped across the fence without a pause
receded on a steep diagonal to a point
in the lower field almost cut off from sight

but there you were again crawling
on a distant hillside now as tiny as a drop
which driven by the sun wobbles blurs and spreads

until released into a heat-haze by a little
gust of air rises to a white cloud and is gone.

LOST IN SOUTH DEVON

You slip out through
the trajectory of your eye –
its path shoots off on a journey
of its own around the room,
settles for a moment lightly
on the floor, describes
a curve and, talking freely now
in conversation with the air,
floats long spiral stories
through the window. Spooling out
your eye unwinds your body
like a ball of string.
It goes about fast and far-flung.
It cruises the possibilities like a dog
let out first thing into the park.
Thought catching sight of thought
and pulling, it locks the mind
into being what it sees.

Now the world is entering your face.
You stare back through the open door
as hard as daylight.
Shining black from last night's rain
your eye walks out abundantly in leaf
along a branch, dwindles
to a narrow stem then disappears
into any tight slit of sky
the green shade lets you through.
Out there you've never been
so pure as this
blank blue racing overhead,
so sharp and pencil-thin
as this horizon. The shoreline

of your body comes, goes, climbs
steep air and curls itself
around clouds. There's no stopping you
lighting on the sea and leaping
dark and blue. Soon you'll be smashing
your head. Down on your knees
you'll be rolling in to the beach
bubbles popping your skin
like the definition of joy.
I want you back – walled
inside your heart, tucked securely
under the covers of your skin.
Keep still inside your given name.
Not this insane unravelling.

THE USUAL THING

The day walks out again
across the earth on cheerful feet.
Here before me the sky unrolls a blue

the length of a calendar with poses
of a blackbird stopping on the path to listen.
The lawn is held transfixed
in spray under the sprinkler system

shiny as a pin-up. The sun,
a bright-eyed boy, is lying on his back
on a sheet of diamonds and yellow silk.

So what does it matter if a branch
drops without warning into the pond
like a slip of the tongue?
If the shadows let out for the night
are hiding like loopholes in the sunshine
in long black ovals under the trees,
if their leaves, already giving up,
bent and broken along the fault lines
of their veins, are letting go in moments
of inattention in the wind or lying
at the end of hope face down on the earth?

The rattle in the poppy's throat
as it issues its message of utterly delicate red
should have aroused my suspicions.

Is it natural for the rose to open
its infant petals so wide,
so perilously far they fall apart and drop
the moment they are born? Tell me again.

The simple action of the day
coming, going, and coming back is a story
I could never quite understand.

BABY'S BREATH

Cut flowers are half-dead
already you said. Shot with milk

the quaking sprays
we'd placed in water rose

in a fathomless curve.
Even the night windows leaned

forward to listen.
The star flowers sharpened.

And while the *Baby's Breath* leapt
in the dark air and hung

poised like a song
broken off half-way through

the clockless seconds stepped
across the floor on tiptoe until

we were bending over the cot
for the least word of your breath

the light sweeping sound of it.
And out of this long dream

we've had of keeping you here
the flowers spread the brief

cloud of their breath
magnified in the dark.

Had they finished opening?
We could see your arms and legs

sprouting with light.
But you were pushing the air

with the crinkled soles of your feet
then vanished at its blue edge.

We sat with our overblown
heads tilted down

dropping petal after petal
onto the carpet under a brown light.

STORY WITH MAGPIES

So it was that the big boys
in a tree moved among the branches.
In black and white like statues

of famous waiters they walked
in their own style with a high
tinselled strut. They paraded

as if they owned the streets
their delicious well-fitting wings.
And out of a blue sky more came

and the tree was blackened and populous
with a great number.
One for sorrow. Two for joy.

And while they flocked and hustled
and the multitude of days and nights
flapped their pages faster in the wind

saying: *this not that, this not that*

one new arrival filed his beak smooth
and dropped you out of the story.

THE DIFFERENCE

after 'The Rock' – Wallace Stevens

It is an illusion that we were ever alive,
that inside you he ever drew a coastline
with his finger and a lake
seen between trees, its loose water

shining with a softness no one could understand.
What was the difference between all the words
for water and the water itself? Out there
sparks lighting it up brought a tree

into flower, a boat tilting a patch of white
carried two people before the wind.
None of this ever happened.
The words spoken, the meeting that lived

in the mind was only an embrace on a beach
between pebbles washed in and out and away.

LIKE THE SEA

An occasional cloud shape hugs
its outlines before letting them go.

The sea comes in again and again
with no colour of its own, only

broken reflections of the sky spread
across the sand. So when a door opened

onto the intolerable white curve
of your back, the surf built

a sturdy white acropolis
then pulled it down like a tent. Or when

I saw you in my mind's eye alert
as a pixie standing in your pyjamas

beside the hospice bed, the memory rose
like the ocean inside a footprint

washing its edges until the wet
slurry was level with the sand.

The sea comes in again and again
with its long tongue and sweeps

across everything I've thought of
washed up on the last tide. It says:

let's stuff all this into an envelope
lick it closed and post it to another country.

AT MILL MEADOW

For a long time she'd slept curled inside
her very shape like an unborn child.

But that day on a walk through the woods
she saw herself open out suddenly

and wide like a long-awaited view to the sea.
And as she flowed away and slid

like the Atlantic over the side of the earth
her body set in motion by the wind

scattered into a field of diamond light.
Atoms flashed on the blue-black bay

like match-heads struck in the dark.
The yes and yes continually repeated

cut her to pieces until she was held
like a swarm of blown flakes dense

as snowfall through which the track is lost.
She runs quickly down the path to the beach

to see it before a cloud
darkens the mob of the senses.

TOMB

He's hidden among the grass – Mallarmé
In all the old familiar places – Billie Holiday

In this new version of yourself
　　　you've abandoned any decent
　　　　　　sense of form and have gone to live openly

in the air – idle as dust
　　　mingling under the bed or casually turning up
　　　　　　in a column of light.

At the moment, I find you floating
　　　at a considerable distance from the ground;
　　　　　　a concentration in the air

has turned you into mist. You are a cloud
　　　moving in the direction of the door,
　　　　　　drifting your face, unravelling your hands,

lifting your fingers on the first breeze.
　　　You slip your edges off just to get away
　　　　　　without saying goodbye.

I'll always think of you that way
　　　even as I listen for a single drop
　　　　　　hard as a grain of rice hitting the street

as innumerable and dark you are growing
　　　so low you obliterate the sky –
　　　　　　then reaching down

your wrecked hands everywhere in gusts
        make accidents happening in the air
                fall wet and silky on my skin.

But I'll find you in the morning sun
        framed against a delicate blue,
                when puddles underfoot sometimes

pull the sky down inside them,
        black circles on the pavement
                deep as mirrors smashed to smithereens.

And when the night is new
        faces flash past station platforms,
                anonymous as leaves blown down the street,

I'll be looking at the moon
        rising to new heights between sheepish clouds
            shrugging their silhouettes,

then sloping off to the horizon random and few
        as so many puffs of dust on the floor,
            But I'll be seeing you.

THE LOGIC OF ATOMS

By the same token as a man
standing in a room is no more
than a busy gathering of atoms

held together by a temporary force,
so the sun shadowed-over
in transit behind a cloud

sends us a tiny signal
of conclusion and we call
after the child going out

in a flash across the kitchen
slamming the back door
Be home before dark. Be home before dark.

And as the man released
from his containing line
gives way like water

longing to be air
the crowd of atoms being
no more than bubbles

crouching on the sides of a pan
about to jump
so we discover he is composed

only as an image in the eye:
restless specks of light
assembled for a moment on the sea

nearly obliterate the boat
with two people
tilting inside him

sails spread before the wind
balancing their weight
against the irreversible.

EVEN WHEN IT SEEMS

Alive even when it seems you are dead
standing behind me when I write
you slip your hand inside mine
as if the skin of my hand were a glove

your fingers inside the tunnels of my fingers
holding the pen. Now it is moving
with a movement so natural it could be
the progress of wind through tall grass,

taking it by force, or it could be a sweet
line of music you've marked *tender* or *fierce*.
Even when it seems you are dead
your hand keeps entering mine, so that when

the idea you are dead
makes a long blank space on the page –
it won't be like hearing
of your death for the first time.

THE CONQUEST OF LOVELESS HILL

There's me climbing
to the precious top.

I've pitched a red tent
as there's still a long way to go –

actually, it's a crevasse.
Glow of raw meat

a hot steaming glow.
Its open mouth

is blooming with hope:
light of an abattoir, the sun

shining at the summit.

CANDLE

after Bachelard

This white dancing spot
in the tiniest drama of matter
flaps like a fish in the air

while someone is holding their breath.
Blinking casually
on its whittled stem

it sends up a lighthouse
with a sort of shrug,
its halo light of arrival

obstinately turning its back.
Eerily free and alone,
but as full of renunciation

as a taxi spotted driving off
down a very dark street,
its self-centred eye

draws night into a circle
around it – a fixed point so far
from the edges of space

it says that no one will ever come.
But, of course, there'll always be someone
nursing a derelict hope –

someone who keeps its single
unclosed eye lit like a chapel
in a field on the outskirts of town.

Even on an airless night someone
will be travelling
through a busy airport anxiously

clutching its hand. When finally
it bends down, curls and blackens,
waves and vanishes into nothing

and the world empties of distance
like the inside of a cupboard,
there'll be someone else

bearing up exceptionally well
as the long clear blue days shove in.

THE SCHOOL FOR DUST

In your millions of no-colour
you make your shapeless debut
at the bottom of a drawer.

I am fully aware that you
accumulate behind the radiator
roll in rough balls and huddle

in secret under beds.
But your little occupations, my dears,
are lower even than yourselves.

For nothing is beneath you.
Your underworld is no deeper
than a teacup and your horizons merely

skim the floor of a dank church.
Do not be deceived by the distinct
shapes you make in the dry places

in deserts and in polluted streets.
I know that you stick to nothing.
You are the epitome of a cloud

the very heart of dispersal.
For yours is the home of failed
epidermis and ineffectual hair

the countless populations too minute
even for gravity to bother with.
So let me hear no more talk

of radiance or eternal life.
A fuzzy shadow on a high shelf
remember, is still and always

the dust of the ground. Example:
just watch how it's formed with water
and a desperate love.

Someone is knitting the soul
gathered from a thousand directions

for one memorable moment before
God help you
unravelled you return to your home.

SUPREME BEING

Let me sit beside you
while you throw your arms around me
like a frame so that animals
and flowers do not spread
across the walls and become too real.

We no longer struggle in a cave
but sit together in a room
and only imagine that a hand
has put down side by side
a rose and a worm
a candle and a wind
a baby and a rushing road.

THE FIRST GAME

I'm playing in my room
        where I'm keeping you on the end of a string

rolled along the tabletop until you fall
        over the edge, under the bed, through the door

down the long hall dwindling out of sight.
        If your head drops below the horizon

of the stairs in a sunset-of-no-return,
        if the Indian Giver comes to take you back

when you've come into the room like a gift,
        if there is always a road waiting

to take you curling round a bend
        like a necklace hurled into a pond

when the water closes over it and swallows it,
        where do your eyes go when they flicker out

peekaboo behind your fingers?
        Where is your face, that thin glimpse

I can make disappear with the slightest
        movement of my head, squeeze half-to-death

or reel out like the line of a song?
        Repeat Repeat
like the long line of a song.

SPECULATIVE POEM

It starts with the only image
that shows up: a flat and featureless blue,
a sky as inattentive and remote
as if a door had slammed. Let's say
the sky is deep in a numb silence
entered only by one or two passing clouds
hanging on the horizon as if
they've stopped for good. Behind them
beats a half-hearted sun playing hell
with the light. Let's say the sky
is a wrecked house ringing and empty
where squatters had once lit a fire.
Floorboards scorched in a black circle,
squashed cans kicked into a corner, a sofa
toppled on its back half-burned. There's even
a dog curled-over studiously licking a cut.
Maybe he belongs to the man I can only see
in silhouette leaning in the open doorway
gazing out. What if his eyes have looked so long
their sight is a tiny begging hand?
Or even better, what if his eyes are rivers
desperate to make it to the sea?
The sumptuous blue is loose and huge,
but always just ahead. Maybe the scrawny water
left crawling in confusion over the stones
has given up the search.
                              And it's the same –
the weather this bad, the feeling I should end it here.
So where does it come from now, this image
of a wind getting up, blowing open a door?
How does the sun become a clasp of light
running across the dark air and distance

of a room? And the clearing blue – why does it now
bend close to a baby sleeping in bed
while I am lying belly-up like open ground
under the sky?

THE PINES

Black girl, black girl, don't lie to me.
Where did you sleep last night?

The moment I fall asleep
I'm in the far corner of her lips

where she keeps her kiss
just out of reach.

What was she hiding inside it?
Her kiss had been slipped

into an envelope and never sent.
It was an enigma handed down

from generation to generation
like the sayings of an old woman.

It was an atlas of the world squeezed
between heavy books on the top shelf.

Her kiss was a hundred coaches long and sped
through the station without stopping.

A fresh twist of the plot, it was always
taking shape on the next page. A wavering

dark road at night wondering where
it would go, it lay restless and waiting

like the black girl who sleeps
in the pines. *In the pines, in the pines*

Where the sun never shines
I shivered the whole night through.

ABOVE THE SURFACE

You streaming fish
rising close to the top of the black pond,
it's you I'll catch on this awakening line

and pull you up from your dark fat world
to the clear slicing element of light.
Here I will part your delicate gills

and pressing my fingers in, your blue
overlapping scales formally composed
and covered in slime I will rake off,

and feeling you wet and dark as you hang
and twist in the slim ecstasy of air
I'll loosen the hook from your mouth

and holding your life between my hands
I'll introduce you to this sleepless
empty space of white.

A GLASS OF MILK

The sun came in through the window
and lay with her there on the bed.
A lit split-second sent

ripples the length of the radiator,
left a glisten on the doorknob,
a knife-edge on the profile of the door,

then with something like a crack
opening the shell of a nut
let in a tall white room.

Its new dimensions sprang
loud and agog with light.

Now following a wrinkle
a fold in the bedclothes makes
into a promise held out and dropped –

a broken line little more
than a stroke of chalk drawn across the dark
runs inside her to a room

parallel to this
where a child is sleeping
set alight by a glass of milk.

SENTENCE

their eyes blow through her as she tries
to speak pad pad pad on mumble feet

her eager as a candle walk
is pulled and wrenched by the wind

their eyes are on her as she tries
to place each wide unwilling

fluent as a puddle word in precisely
the right slippery order on the floor

their eyes are vacant air around her
as she tries to balance teeter totter high

Look she is forming a sentence!
on a single long tightropey line

heading babystep babystep
for a silence waiting

without hands
on the other side of the room

ANECDOTE OF A STONE

Dull and exact as a stone
this word might have remained
in the kingdom of minerals
the colour of grey iron and obedient
to its cold law if I hadn't
bent down to find it
just the right size for my hand
if I hadn't lifted it from the dust
by the side of the road
and aimed it unswerving as a key
and while the pond lay perfectly still
locked edge to edge in the ground
flat as a cloth covering a table
or a face that gave nothing away
it's as if this one word
with the piercing trajectory of a stone
sailed through the air
and if this could have been
the accomplishment of a stone
it might have rung
in the high air like a bell
it might have waved a flag at the sky
and while the pond lay
huddled in a dark circle
holding its deep breath like a wish
this word might have leant
close as a stone and bent
its long black arc down
and if the pond had held open its centre
its target as wide as an ear
listening this one word might
with the accuracy of a stone
have broken the surface with a gentle splash

and found its way to the abundant
unentered heart beating at the bottom
and even though the pond had withdrawn
to an innermost place pulled back
like a house behind its walls
it's as if this one word
rode straight through its doors
and sent the awakened waves
curling and casting their light
in increasing circles
like a smile that won't stop
breaking across your face.

THE GEODE

Listen well to the stone:
it releases its bang in the dust
like a statement of fact.

But let's make this
blunt stone into a brain.
Let's make its small

geography light up
like Vienna at twilight
in an ambience of meadows and emerald air.

Let's make it into a honeycomb
of yellow streetlit squares and angled
courtyards celled in quiet.

The eye is speechless
as it moves among the resplendent
many-sided gabled houses

and crystal-pointed chimneys
pushed up one by one
like pencils

where even a geologist
meditating
over a packet of cigarettes

would be lost
in the cobbled back streets
of the intelligence.

BRINK

Over warm brown windows night
like a sea leaning down
rolls in to cover the house

heavily with its black length.
Battened down in a milky calm
blinds pulled tight

I prepare the tea and wait
in the dark kitchen.
Outside the paths taper quickly

away to touch a line of light.
The kettle pounds and begins
to exhale its bubbles.

The house a tiny hero
pauses upright
on the edge of the night.

THE WILD DUCK IN THE ATTIC

When our minds have shut their doors
the rooms hum as if the house,
eyes closed, rests sideways

on a pillow dreaming, each chink
half-open like a mouth.
Dreamer, we thought we knew your body

like an alphabet we'd learned by heart:
the dark places wedged
like blood under a thumbnail,

a crescent of shadow
in the fold of a cupboard,
the skeletal elbow of the stairs bending,

your skin so transparent it's like
two inches of tap water in the bath.
But now all that matters is the light –

the sharp slit under the attic door
rushing forward, thin white arms open
wide enough to hold an auditorium,

while we, suspending disbelief,
sink down in our seats to watch
the house begin to swing

around its mooring like a boat.
In the shifting wind
the attic door blows open like a shining example.

And now we're seeing that other place
twilit as the underside of the sea.
We're seeing where the wild duck lies

the colour of water hiding at the bottom,
in a new kind of drowning.
Nothing is less certain than this

vast handkerchief of ocean rumpled
by the wind, this low miniature sky
the wild duck dabbling her orange feet,

looping her neck in thought under her wing.
Breathe your secret breath, wild duck,
like a god in the dark.

THE VOICE OF THE MOON

I'm going to sit right down and write myself a letter
And make-believe it came from you – Fats Waller

I'm writing from a distance impossible
to imagine, yet you imagine it.

You can picture clearly the precise
angle of my face, head on my hand,

glancing down when you come into the room.
You can picture the intent long look

when I ask – *What form will it take?*
Or when I say – *Stay faithful to me.*

You have only to wait. All night long I'm here
in and out between sliding moods and clouds

so far off only an astronomer's trained eye
could see, but I'm plainly visible

sitting in a high mineral room domed and lit
like an exciting foreign capital at night.

Or catch sight of me through the window
no clearer than an inkling:

a circle drifting in the hazy
unplumbed depths of an animal brain.

I'll enter in sharp definition
like a bright idea in a cone of light

and rest my pensive head in my hands.
Or picture me deep inside

the body of a cave sealed in sleep.
I'll be the energetic hermit

going about his routine business
knocking loudly as a heart.

And if you could travel to the far
reaches of my face

where my mouth forms a secret O
there's the small illuminated scene

locked away, where you fondly imagine
I'm thinking of you.

A CONCISE HISTORY OF ART

As if taking the room's slant on things
he snaps her face and hair into the space

between the yellow formica worktop and the door.
Or moving her a little forward, long

and permanent as a peninsula
she reaches out to touch the handle of a cup.

But details such as these are quite superfluous.
He keeps her to the minimum of what she is.

One black outline will suffice.
Her crescent profile with its single eye,

iconic as a billboard, hovers in the air:
flat, reliable and Egyptian.

But see how she begins – how she receives
a slight twist at the waist,

how one foot steps out, the high
degree of relief of her fingers. Vistas

open up and rush away, oblique lines
lengthen and discover convergence.

She shortens as she leaves through the door,
half-hidden, half-gone. But then, as she arrives,

she is larger! Your complete attention.
Surely, that's a smile.

Now her body leads a double life,
full of prepositions: *in* and *out*

and especially *around* – her back as lost
to sight as the dark part of the moon.

Her glowing head is tilting forward.
Silent upon the slope of her cheek

he has come to the outermost rim of the visible.
Down the slack line of her arm, past her elbow

there's her hand opening a grassy path
where his eye goes barefoot,

while he sets out like a medieval saint
into the empty quarter, glancing up to peer

across the hilly distance
with a parcel over his shoulder.

ELEVEN

In those days she had wide sunlit parkland
under her boy's T-shirt
bleached and smooth as a timber plank.

As if she'd been born to run her hands
barefoot through the clear acres
of early morning and the great blonde fields

she carried it everywhere: the proud
expanse of her chest bare and serene as a scalp.
But to arrive like this! Camped

on the slope of a hill – a gypsy tent
like a strange brown bud beginning
to poke from a tree. At nightfall now

under the noisy dome of her shirt
the big top presents a turmoil of acts.
In the steep bleachers she's gazing down,

in one hand popcorn, in the other a goldfish,
at a two-ringed circus spotlit in the purple dark.
From puddles of light the size of a thumb

jump twin pink creatures arrogant as fruit.
She walks, she talks, she wriggles
on her belly like a reptile!

The uncloaked dancers rise to focal points
ravishing the crowd
and move as if they entertain

a distant project no one could foresee
in the brilliant sawdust: they build
fat pyramids that look enormously small.

And these two acrobats, each exhibiting
a dark pink tutu like a nimbus
in the tiny distance, smiling, bowing,

while still tossing from hand to hand
a bowling ball and an egg,
weigh her down, weigh her down.

FAÇADE

Seen from the back prominent and alone
brooding at the kitchen sink
it seemed your body stood
on the crest of a hill with the long

patience of public architecture, Paladian
wings stretching down to the water,
a great building with the silence
of a face about to speak.

Even from this distance we could see
it had ideas of its own mapped
inside it, arched colonnades and shrines
lonely as the pockets in a lung.

Taciturn as a church, your body
did not speak. You spoke from it.
As words rose from your lips, starlings
erupted in a rustling swarm and flew.

Sometimes we could see a pale
brown window late at night,
the eye you looked out of, leading back
along a hallway to the festivities inside

hidden as the fingers of two hands
humming like a congregation
clasped together in a fist.
Here is the church. Here is the steeple.

But we had to imagine you
saying your prayers, a bent figure
kneeling in the tall nave
of yourself, an empty religious space

going up to the roof. Tonight
your body, a solid block gliding
in movement into the room,
is as watchful and withdrawn as a prison.

The population, the hundreds
detained at Her Majesty's pleasure,
holed up in the outline of a man
are rattling the bars of their cells.

ONLY FOR A MOMENT

A grey sky and a stone
hurled into its great grey face –
a stone in the air which never

returns to the ground.
Promise me you will come back
a tree says to its broken
October leaves going brown.

The earth swings into its long
orbit away from the sun like a toy
a child squatting in a corner flings

so hard it snaps
the end of its string or perhaps

the sun has only gone for a moment
behind a cloud as if it were asleep.

FALL

You with your compact skin worn tight
around you like the bark hugging a tree
or gathered to you like a garden wall

at one with yourself and singular
fooled me into thinking that a man
standing in a room could not lengthen

and crumble like a leaf or break
as if a wind blew fiercely through his flesh
but you fell from the tall level of your face

as easily as if you had just opened your shirt.

SPRING

may be no more than a thought
that occurred to me once last year

in February when a tuft of green grass
showed through a hole in the snow

as if you'd held out your sparse hands
to thaw and might return.

IF IT DIE

Now he's been laid deep in a drawer among
the forgotten washers and paperclips
he's gone brown as an unread letter

whose words lie curled up in bed
asleep. Tight as stones their eyes are closed
and will not open. It is February again

in her mind when they begin. Twigs
inching out from under the bedclothes like children
– heads coming into bud. They poke out long

unwrinkled stalks and wave them in the air
a bare leg, a bare arm, a bare leg.
They throw back the covers and tasting them

on her quick tongue she is leaping
out loud through her mouth
knowing that this is herself unhidden.

COULD YOU NOT

kiss me your wonderful kiss
upside-down in a world where you make
your tongue into a tree my eye

climbs straight to the top to find
such green branches tossing
a circle into the sky

that I shrink to the size of a baby
crammed with the enormous milk?

A MIND OF WINTER

for Wallace Stevens in March

Silenced and sent outside
as if the world was a child
he wanted out of the room
the view from the window showed
only those cold thoughts
that tended to comply with white

a glaring region where his mind
took hold of trees and bent
their shoulders until they sighed
made them sag knee-deep
here and there like melted candles
stuck to a table in an empty house

and glowing like a pearl
placed a hard white sun low
in a windswept sky imagining his own
small face on a pillow in a new-made bed
then becoming one white quiet thing

draped thick blankets across his knees
so that the book he held
lightly in his hand was spread
open to a page where the icy
scene was set pitiless and horizontal

until his footprint gaping open in the snow
became a shape he no longer recognised
letting through a patch of green
and it was like a holiday
he'd been looking forward to for months
and a keyhole to the heart.

RABBIT AND WIND

The indifferent wind comes
to collect you in its arms.

You bend your papery head,
nod and sway before the wind sweeps

across the dry field your body has become

where, in the late morning
the sun still half-asleep cracks open

a blue eye behind a procession of clouds
where, in the rough stubble and dirt,

is the first hint of a rabbit.

The wind is a clown and speaks gibberish,
performs feats in the air, balances

a kitchen chair on a tightrope, runs through
a list of things without stopping. The wind says

You are as valuable as a pebble.
You should wear it around your neck.

You say to the rabbit

Go Rabbit – and take me with you.
Leave behind that aspect of myself

I can only do alone.

PORTRAIT FROM MEMORY

You sit in what remains
of an eye, the joking gesture of a hand.
Your back has a straight long look
the elements attack and wear away
leaving a little less each year.

A little less still wears your face.
The story is weaker, told to hold
you in a net. It takes minutes
to unpick the outline of a ruined arm,
the scant reminder of a smile.
A little less is certain in the mind.

Even a sentence lets its objects scatter,
the movement trees are making in their leaves.
The flesh of earth becomes the flesh of air.
Every little breeze seems to whisper Louise
a little less is saying.

A stone would not lie
more quietly
in this niche than you
up to your neck in shadow.

The little of your face
points north
its profile
having let you go

now encloses a lesser
shape lessening
and less
tapped into craters by the wind.

Water collects
in the pitted granite
of your nose and mouth.
Lid open blindly

to the weather
your grey eye is a cloud
trapped at the bottom
of a cup of rain.

How can it not rush out
in all
possible directions
into the happening colour?

Parting the tight hills
just in time
to catch
a long blue stream

swinging ahead
like a child
this way and that
in the lime-green valley

it might have made
heavy uncut fields of grass
leap and wave
in the light sun.

It might have read
the brown
dotted surfaces of ferns
like Braille.

SNOW

This new weather opens
on a silent hinge with you

as its famous protagonists.
In a blizzard of a hundred

demeanours you people the air
with the many white

gestures your body
made in room after room

darkening on the stairs
throwing a door open

to the light, striding in
bending gently over a bed.

The storm turns inland.
The large white flakes fall.

Each one stars your face
dissolving on the road.

They pause for a mild unmoving
moment of celebrity

hovering like the one or two
desultory pictures

in the paper I'm leafing through
on my way to work.